Discovering True Identity

The Believer's Position in Christ
Freedom Series: Volume One

F. Dean Hackett, Ph.D.

 SPIRIT LIFE MINISTRIES INTERNATIONAL

Spirit Life Ministries International

Discovering True Identity
Copyright © 2012 by F. Dean Hakcett, Ph.D.

This title is also available as an ebook. Visit
www.fdeanhackett.com/store

Requests for information should be addressed to Spirit
Life Ministries Publications, Hermiston, Oregon 97838

ISBN: 978-0615733258

Cover design: Stephanie Eidson
Cover photography: Pixabay
Interior Design: Rosilind Jukić

Printed in the United States of America

I dedicate this work to my dear mother, Mary J. Swanby who encouraged my graduate studies and writing; and now watches from Heaven's portal.

Contents

Preface

The demand for relevancy and dynamic ministry is being placed upon the Church of Jesus Christ with renewed vigor. Overwhelming social conflict; the breakdown of human relationships; and the earthquake of emotions flooding our society are crying out as the Children Israel under the inhuman slavery of Egypt.

The daily pressures of living with broken relationships and pent-up emotions of anger, bitterness and hate are convulsing individual's lives. The attack by a 15-year-old boy in the cafeteria of Thurston High School, Springfield, Oregon is merely one example of human lives exploding out of control.

The deterioration of a child's well-being over the past four decades is one of our most tragic domestic treads. The Council on Families in America reported in 1995, "Never before has one generation of American teenagers been less healthy, less cared for, or less prepared for life than their parents were at the same age."

Violence in the streets has reached pandemic proportions. Gangs war for claimed territories. Men, women, boys and girls rob and kill for the next fix. Social ills and STD bring to our medical services unprecedented demands. Political, media and education resources continue to pressure for acceptance of the alternative life style of homosexuals, lesbians, transvestites and bi-sexual couples. Education reform and political correctness are rewriting history and moral values.

These human dilemmas require resources and skills for ministry here-to-fore unknown in this generation. It is in this fire-storm of cultural eruption a Child

1

of God can make their finest stand. We cannot afford to be irrelevant, monastic or indifferent at such an hour in human history.

We cannot allow ourselves to be like Samson in the Old Testament. He was stripped of power tied to a grinding wheel and walking in circles. Our source of power and relevance is found in the sufferings of Jesus Christ. His agonizing prayer in the garden, betrayal, arrest, flogging, death, burial and resurrection are the only sources of hope and victory for the current human dilemma.

Some well-meaning sociologists and religious leaders may think this culturally irrelevant and simplistic. However, in the trenches of societal war zones it has been proven often to be the only source of dynamic power that changes the heart of a devastated life. The resurrection power of Jesus Christ has shown to be the greatest source of deliverance from alcoholism, drug addiction and violent crime. When all other sources of help have failed, the life-changing power of the cleansing blood of Jesus Christ has been the dynamic that can heal a broken marriage, restore a run-away child, or reconcile a gang war.

This study examines intently what Jesus Christ has done to win such a victory for every person. It will also discuss the role a disciple of Jesus Christ has in ministering that victory to the crisis of our generation. The victory Jesus Christ has won conquers the power of sin and delivers from temptation in daily living. It gives victory over death and hell in eternity.

His victory has the power to transform the hardest heart to accomplish the impossible. No crisis is too great and no circumstance too extreme. There is no life irreversibly destroyed by sin. No relationship is so crushed by the power of hate, bitterness and abuse that it cannot be healed. Jesus' power is greater.

Rejoice!
Christ has won the victory!

God's Original Design

When God created mankind He placed them in a beautiful paradise, the Garden of Eden. In this paradise Adam and Eve experienced full and unhindered fellowship with God. They lived within the divine protection of their Creator and experienced the gracious provision of His bounty and love.

Adam was given authority to be the steward of all God had created.

> *"And God blessed them, and God said unto them, be fruitful and multiply, and replenish the earth, and subdue it: And have dominion over the fish of the sea, and over the fowl of the air, and over every living thing that moveth upon the earth" (Genesis 1:28 KJV).*

The extent of Adam's authority is revealed in Psalm 8:4-9 and Hebrews 2:5-8. "You have put all things under his feet… He left nothing that is not put under him." Adam's authority to rule the earth was so complete he had the responsibility of naming all the animals and creatures God created. "An out of the ground the Lord God formed every beast of the field and every fowl of the air; and brought them unto Adam to see what he would call them: And whatsoever Adam called every living creature, that was the name thereof" (Genesis 2:19 KJV). He even had the privilege of naming his wife. "Adam said, this is now bone of my bone and flesh of my flesh: She shall be called Woman, because she was taken out of man" (Genesis 2:23).

What an amazing and wonderful relationship God planned for his man and woman. They lived with Him in open relationship filled with intimacy and perfect love. Their marriage relationship gave affirmation, encouragement and companionship. Love was pure and wholesome. They had the privilege of being caretakers of God's perfect creation. All of this was enjoyed in a perfect environment free from anxiety, guilt, fear, hate, bitterness, jealousy, rejection, insecurity, envy, or low self-worth. This was the life to be lived eternally by the human race.

The joy of this continued paradise and exalted state of living was predicated upon the obedience of Adam and Eve. God gave clear and explicit instructions. "Any tree of the garden you may eat freely; but from the tree of the knowledge of good and evil you may not eat, for in the day that you eat from it you will surely die" (Genesis 2:16-17 NAS).

God wanted Adam to understand the basis of living in the image of God and having the authority to rule over creation. Adam had the eternal privilege. However, if he ever transgressed and partook of the forbidden fruit all would be lost and he would certainly die.

The certainty of those instructions and the consequence of disobedience were lost upon Adam and Eve in the blind fog of temptation. Spiritual vertigo set in upon them. The first couple committed the unthinkable. The results of the transgression were unbelievably swift and irreversible. It always is. The violator seldom takes into consideration the irretrievable loss of a serpentine act.

Adam and Eve learned only too quickly the deadly consequences of their violation. Genesis 3:7-24 records the grievous events that followed their yielding to temptation. The immediate loss of innocence and the covering of God's glory brought a vain attempt to cover their shame and nakedness with fig leaves. Their guilty conscience drove them into hiding from the presence of God, their Father, and the sweet fellowship they had previously enjoyed. Self-justification produced blame-shifting and a denial of their personal responsibility.

Nothing said or done could reverse the damage brought upon the human race, marriage and family relationships, and planet earth. The judgment of God was pronounced upon all involved: the serpent, the woman, the man, and the earth.

Paradise was lost.

The final and the most severe penalty came when God removed the couple from the Garden of Eden. He set a flaming sword and Cherubim to guard the entrance. Never again would Adam and his offspring enjoy the security and the provision of the Garden. Never again would they have the companionship and the fellowship with Almighty God so openly enjoyed previously.

There was an even greater loss yet to be experienced by this couple. It was a loss they could never have envisioned while standing by the forbidden tree.

Cain and Able were the sons of Adam and Eve. They were vastly different, as in most cases. Able was a shepherd. Cain was a farmer. Cain was very jealous of his little brother. Jealousy turned to hate. Hate led to rage. Rage took Cain to murder.

When word arrived of Abel's death, at the hands of his brother, it must have been a crushing blow to these dear parents. Any question in the mind of

Adam and Eve about the continuum of their sin was now answered. The horror of their son's act was only the fruit of their first sin.

> *"Wherefore as by one man's sin entered into the world, and death*
> *by sin, and so death passed upon all men for all have sinned"*
> *(Romans 5:12 KJV).*

The agony and pain experienced by the first couple has been a continual pain to every couple since that day. Every parent has felt the pain of sin's sting as they watch their children wrestle with the curse of sin.

There is no human being on earth who escapes grip of sin. The certainty and the reality of sin are seen immediately in the heart of a child who demands their own way. It grows with each passing day. As the children into adulthood, the childish demands for feeding and attention become adult demands for power, control, money and sex.

It is the expression of this sin that fills city streets with violence. It is sin that steals the security of children having two parents in the home. It is sin that takes advantage of defenseless little girls. Sin drives needles into the arms of the craving. Sin fills magazines with nudity and sells vice on street corners. Sin gnaws in the avaricious heart of a corporate executive. Sin explodes in the violence of an angry teenager.

Whether it is a small child stealing candy from a corner store or a Wall Street broker embezzling millions from an investment firm, it is sin that fills the heart. It is sin in the heart of every person of every race, nation and tongue. That is why God declared, "There is none righteous, no not one… For all have sinned and come short of the glory of God" (Romans 3:10, 23 KJV).

The consequence of sin is devastating to the human race. This was Lucifer's plan from the time he entered the Garden to tempt Eve. His plan was three fold. He wanted to steal man's authority as stewards over creation so he could be the god of this world. He was out to kill human dignity and worth and the image of God within mankind. He sought to destroy mankind's relationship with God and with one another.

Through this plan he could enslave human beings to sin and the dominion of his kingdom of darkness. The slavery of people to the kingdom of darkness is the source of every ill and corruption that plagues the human race.

The Apostle John defined it well.

> "Love not the world, neither the things that are in the world. If any man love the world, the love of the Father is not in him. For all that is in the world, lust of the flesh, and the lust of the eyes, and the pride of life, is not of the Father, but is of the world" (1 John 2:15-17 KJV).

The Apostle John articulated the three core problems every person will deal with in life. Whether they live in the Chinese culture, Croatian culture or Canadian culture, whether the person lived in 2000 BC, AD 100, or 2012, every person deals with the lust of the flesh, the lust of the eyes and the pride of life.

These three core issues have been the driving force behind Alexander the Great, Adolf Hitler, Mao Tse-tung and Saddam Hussein. They are the motivation of Hollywood, Las Vegas and the Mexican Drug Cartel. These three are the underlying cause of anorexia, alcoholism, drug addiction, and teen suicide. They are the force behind marital unfaithfulness, child abuse and divorce.

Lust of the flesh is the driving force of sexual desire whether it is pre-marital sex (fornication), extra-marital sex (adultery) or perversion (homosexual, transsexual, and all unnatural forms of sexual behavior).

Lust of the eyes is greed. Greed is not just Donald Duck's Uncle Scrooge hording his money. Greed is placing my self-worth and my security in anything other than God.

Pride of Life is self-directed living; Scripture calls it iniquity. It is self-willed living, having the final redress; being a self-made individual. When hurt or wronged they hold the account and will not forgive. If they do forgive, they cannot forget.

The story for mankind does not end in despair, even though World War I did not end all wars and World War II did not put an end to all dictatorships and aggression. There is hope for mankind even though we see the continual rise of terrorism and pandemic crime and moral breakdown.

When God pronounced judgment after the fall of Adam and Eve, He gave a powerful and a thrilling promise.

> *"And I will put enmity between thee [the Serpent] and the woman;*
> *and between thy seed and her seed; and it shall bruise thy head and*
> *thou shalt bruise his heel" (Genesis 3:15 KJV).*

This is an amazing assurance from Heavenly Father. Satan won that day in the Garden. But, there was another day coming. There was another Garden experience in the future. The day would come when God would bring forth the seed of woman and He would destroy the works of the Kingdom of Satan. He would deliver mankind from the slavery of sin and the oppression of darkness. He would restore that which had been destroyed. He would give life to that which had been killed. He would return what had been stolen. As Paul Harvey would say, "That is the rest of the story."

To the Victor Go the Spoils

Tears filled his eyes as he looked longingly out the back window of the family car. His mother was driving him and his sisters away from their home, and their dad. On the backdoor steps of their house, the father stood crying and begging the mother not to leave.

 The car did not stop. The pain in the heart of that five-year-old boy grew deeper as he watched the image of his papa fade and disappear. Standing in the backseat, looking out the back window, he made a vow, a vow that would bring years of pain and sorrow. A seed of bitterness was planted in his heart that day. The seed sprouted and began a defiling work that would grow each year and corrupt his young life. The bitterness in his heart caused many years of grief for his family and sent him on a downward spiral of disastrous consequences.

One can hardly imagine a five-year-old having a downward-spiraling life. It is true. Far too many children start life in the whirlpool of bitterness. The swirling pool of sin began in this young boy's life with the introduction of pornography and sexual abuse at age six. The sexual abuse continued multiple times a week for seven years. By nine years of age, his anger was out of control and violence was becoming more and more a pattern of his behavior. He was smoking in the third grade and could embarrass adults with his foul language.

At eleven, he almost killed another boy in a fit of rage. A man walking by stopped him before he plunged a pair of lawn clippers into the boy's heart.

13

He entered the eighth grade having failed every year of school up to that time. He was addicted to pornography and had hardened his heart with a vow to never cry again.

When he was fifteen he could not remember feeling loved. He thought himself to be the most ugly and unlovable person on planet earth. He had no self-worth and was an inferno of hate and violence. He would have explosions of unexplainable rage, even when alone. The only moments of happiness would come when he was singing or playing sports. But, if he lost the game, there would be long periods of depression and feelings of failure and worthlessness.

The story of this boy is a classic example of the trauma and pain sin has wrecked upon the human existence. The result of Adam's fall in the Garden of Eden has not diminished with the millennia of time. History is the story of mankind's struggle with the results of that disaster and the reality that "time does not heal all wounds."

There is good news! History also documents God's miraculous work of reconciliation. God has not left man to his own devices and struggle to figure it out. God has entered the human fray and made a way for every human being to be delivered from the rags and torture of sinful abusive living.

Satan uses many tools to perpetrate his vile and destructive schemes. He lures the natural appetites of the flesh with tantalizing temptations. He oppresses a person's mind will and emotions with fear, worry, anxiety, frustration, jealousy, envy and other negative feelings. Through these weapons he suppresses life and seeks to enslave the individual to the kingdom of darkness.

Scripture instructs us regarding his tactics and weaponry. We are commanded to clothe ourselves carefully with the armor of God so we can withstand his subtle attacks. An examination of Satan's tools and weaponry would be in order.

The enemy of mankind uses four primary battle plans. They are deception, strongholds, temptation and intimidation. Each device is used to enter into an individual's life so Satan can steal, kill and destroy.

Deception is a covert operation whereby the powers of darkness seek to trap an unsuspecting victim by using lies, half-truths and distortion. A person living under deception has no idea they are deceived. The enemy is able to do his covert work unhindered. Once the person discovers they are living under deception they have opportunity to be made free. Jesus said, "And ye shall know the truth and the truth shall make you free" (John 8:32 KJV).

The serpent deceived Eve in the Garden of Eden using partial truth and distorting questions. He used Scripture out of context and misleading questions to tempt Jesus in the wilderness. Satan's oily tongue asked, "If you are the Son of God…" Deceptively he proclaimed, "It is written…" (Matthew 4:3-4 NIV). Satan uses these devices with craft and stealth yet today. It is imperative we live alert or we will fall just as the original couple fell.

Strongholds are areas in the mind, will, emotions and flesh controlled by the powers of darkness. The Apostle Paul taught the Church at Corinth:

> *"For though we walk (live) in the flesh, we are not carrying on our warfare according to the flesh and using mere human weapons. For the weapons of our warfare are not physical (weapons of flesh and*

blood), but they are mighty before God for the overthrow and
destruction of strongholds, [In as much as we] refute arguments and
theories and reasoning and every proud and lofty thing that sets itself
up against the (true) knowledge of God, and we lead every thought
and purpose away captive into the obedience of Christ, the Messiah,
the Anointed one" (2 Corinthians 10:3-5 AMP).

The Apostle Paul also warned the Ephesian church to be careful about giving the enemy a foothold. "In your anger," he wrote, "Do not sin: Do not let the sun go down while you are still angry, and do not give the devil a foothold" (Ephesians 4:26-27 NIV). Literally, do not give the enemy an area of jurisdiction.

Ed Silvoso describes the concept in his excellent volume *That None Should Perish.*

> *"A spiritual stronghold is a mind-set impregnated with hopelessness*
> *that causes us to accept as unchangeable, situations that we know*
> *are contrary to the will of God" (Regal, 1994, p. 155).*

The Apostle understood the great risk involved when a person gives the powers of darkness authority over an area of their life. The dark forces will seize the opportunity to torment and afflict the person with every sort of mental, emotional and physical torture. The enemy is seeking to harass the individual to the point of suppressing their thoughts, emotions and will to the point they are able to gain greater and greater control of the person's life, even to the point of ownership.

It is incumbent upon us to carefully guard our heart and mind from those opportunistic forces seeking to gain territorial rights within our life.

Temptations attack the natural appetites of the body. Abraham Maslow's Theory of sex, sleep, homeostasis and excretion describe this hierarchy of natural appetites. While this is true in the natural sense, the enemy of mankind seeks to use these basic needs as opportunity to steal, kill and to destroy. The Holy Scriptures describes it very well.

"But every man is tempted when he is drawn away of his own lust and enticed" (James 1:14 KJV).

Temptations lure through the eye gate and draw the appetites of the flesh, urging the individual to use the drives God has given them in a selfish and unlawful manner. Jesus painted the picture clearly in His Sermon on the Mount.

"If thy right eye offend thee, pluck it out, and cast if from thee…
And if thy right hand offend thee, cut it off, and cast it from thee"
(Matthew 5:29-30 KJV).

Jesus was painting a word picture using an animal trap to describe temptation. The Greek word for "offend" is *skandalizei*. It references the foot of an animal trap, where the bait is placed to lure the prey. When the creature reaches for the tantalizing feast the *skandalizei* trips the snare. That is the danger of temptation pulling at the natural appetites of the flesh. Commercials, magazine covers, movies and music are ever seeking to lure our flesh into the enemy's *skandalizei*.

"Each one is tempted when, by his own evil desire, he is dragged away and enticed. Then, after desire has conceived, it gives birth to

sin; and sin, when it is full-grown, gives birth to death. Don't be
deceived, my dear brothers" (James 1:14-16 NIV).

Intimidation is the vile effort of the wicked forces to control a person through fear. The famous *fop* and *fos* are the tools used to work on the mind and emotions to enslave a person through the *fear of people* and the *fear of success*.

The dark powers will use the weapons of dominating personalities, positions of power, anger, abusive language, manipulative speech, and controlling emotions to intimidate and control another person to the point that person is held hostage to the wishes and demands of the controlling personality.

It may be an employer who uses negative motivation or a parent who uses name calling or anger to coerce their child. Self-pity and manipulative emotions are often used by a marriage partner or a sibling to get their way. This kind of manipulation is demeaning and damages a person's spirit. The powers of darkness will use these behavior patterns to shape the thought life and emotions of an individual to build a stronghold. The enemy's objective is to make that person a POW in the spiritual war between the Kingdom of God and the Kingdom of Darkness.

Fear of success is another mighty tool in the enemy's arsenal. He will use accusation (real or imagined), past mistakes and failures to torment the mind and suppress the emotions. That is why he is called "the accuser of the brethren... which accused them before our God day and night" (Revelation 12:10 KJV).

He will fill the mind with accusing memories of past sins and former life-styles to impede spiritual growth and advancement. He will enliven failure and weaknesses to remind a person why they cannot take that promotion or succeed in a new position. He will flood the heart with feelings of condemnation and moral weakness to prevent them from believing God could use them to accomplish anything for the Kingdom of God.

The most diabolical work of intimidation happens during trauma. Preying upon the innocent and unsuspecting, he will take advantage of pain-filled events to accomplish his dirty work.

The individual cannot control these circumstances and is very vulnerable. Much like a burglary, the powers of darkness seek entrance into the victim's life during a traumatic experience. Trauma will leave a person open to fear, worry, rejection, insecurity and other negative emotions. Satan will seek to capitalize on these opportunities.

The evil forces will seize moments of terror in a natural disaster, auto accident, a fall or recreational accident. He will take advantage of horrible events such as rape, molestation, and physical abuse to gain a foothold and build a stronghold in the mind and emotions of the person.

Satan has a definite agenda in his work of deception, temptation, strongholds and intimidation. He is ever seeking to oppress, suppress, obsess and possess human lives. It is always with the objective to destroy the God-given purpose and destiny of a person.

He will seek to oppress an individual with the goal of suppressing their mind, will and emotions. Once the forces of darkness have suppressed the spirit of an individual they will seek to control them through obsessive behavior.

Oppressed emotions become the controlling and the dominating force in their life. The sinful experience that was once so gratifying becomes a life-controlling habit.

Now held captive by their own emotions or by the habits they once practiced for pleasure, the person has become a prisoner of the powers of darkness. How very true are the words of the Apostle Paul. "Do you not know that to whom you present yourselves slaves to obey, you are that one's slave whom you obey, whether of sin leading to death or of obedience leading to righteousness" (Romans 6:16 NKJV)?

There is only one anecdote for the bondage and slavery holding mankind. It is not political reform, social engineering, better education, psychotherapy, or another twelve step program. Freedom from slavery of the heart requires a greater source of power.

The Bane of Bitterness

I stood before the woman, waiting in prayer for clarity from God. She had responded to the altar call, seeking the laying on of hands and anointing of oil for physical healing. As I waited, the Holy Spirit began to impress upon me a deeper need and a more important need than the back pain for which she came for prayer. This dear woman of God had suffered for years. The pain was almost disabling at times. It seemed God opened the heavens and allowed me to see into the spirit realm. This woman was afflicted with a spirit of infirmity. The affliction had come upon on her because she was bitter. I gently inquired, "May I ask you a question?" "Yes," was her tearful response. "What family member are you bitter against," was my question. She broke into deep sobs, tears flood from her eyes. "My son," She exclaimed. "He has deeply hurt me." I paused so she could have a few moments to sorrow. Then I asked, "Are you willing to forgive him? Right now! Will you release all judgment and accountability against him, for what he has done to you?" "Oh, yes," she sobbed. With that, she began praying exuberantly. After a few moments of earnest prayer, she suddenly cried out, "It's gone! The pain is gone!" That wonderful healing did not diminish with time. I saw her several years later and she was still rejoicing in the healing received that morning.

The writer of Hebrews explained, "Follow peace with all men, and holiness, without which no one shall see the Lord" (Hebrews 12:14 KJV). The Amplified version records the verse, "Strive to live in peace with everybody, and pursue that consecration and holiness, without which no one will [ever] see the Lord."

Clear instructions are being given by the Hebrew writer regarding the joy and future hope of living eternally with God in His Kingdom. However, there is a broader application. If a person is going to see God and His glory involved in their life on a day to day basis they also must "strive to live thereby many be defiled: lest there be any fornicator, peace with everybody and pursue that consecration and holiness…" That is the broader application of the context.

"Looking diligently lest any man fail of the grace of God; lest any root of bitterness springing up trouble you, and thereby many be defiled; lest there be any fornicator, or profane person as Esau, who for one morsel of meat sold his birth right. For you know how that afterward, when he would have inherited the blessing, he was rejected: For he found no place of repentance, though he sought it carefully with tears" (Hebrews 9:15-17 KJV).

When a person fails to guard their heart from unforgiveness they plant a seed. A root of bitterness will grow from that seed, infecting the heart. It is impossible to keep the infection from spreading, "and the many become contaminated and defiled by it" (Hebrews 12:15 AMP). The cost of unforgiveness and bitterness is so great; no one can afford to pay the price.

The Apostle Paul gave important instructions regarding this matter. "In your anger, do not sin, do not let the sun go down while you are still angry, and do not give the devil a foothold" (Ephesians 4:26-27 NIV). Notice the connection between unresolved anger and giving the devil an opportunity to establish his kingdom and jurisdiction. When a person allows unresolved conflict to remain overnight, the enemy takes advantage and establishes territorial rights in that area of their life. The Greek word translated "foothold" (NIV) or "place" (KJV) in Ephesians 4:27 is *topos*. Kenneth Wuest gives the following definition in his *Word Studies in the Greek New Testament, Ephesians and Colossians.*

> *"Any portion of space marked off from the surrounding territory.'*
> *Here it is used in the sense of opportunity, power, occasion for*
> *acting" (1973, p. 114).*

Describing the tense of the Greek grammar Wuest says:

> *'Neither give place' is in a construction in Greek which forbids the*
> *continuance of an action already going on. It is literally, 'and stop*
> *giving place.'"*

The warning is so clear. Do not allow any day to end with unresolved conflict or anger. When you do the enemy of your souls will have an opportunity. Like a burglar, he will come into your life and begin plundering.

Jesus gave a very descriptive teaching on the cost of bitterness. The Apostle Peter asked Him an important question about forgiveness. "Lord how often shall my brother sin against me and I forgive him" (Matthew 18:21)? We all need the answer to that question.

Jesus responded, "Four hundred and ninety times." Then he taught the disciples a parable saying, "There is the kingdom of heaven likened unto…" (Matthew 18:23). The story is about a man who owed a tremendous debt of approximately ten million dollars. He begged forgiveness of the one to whom he owed the debt and it was granted.

The forgiven man also had a debtor. Approximately one hundred days' wages were owed to him, an insignificant amount compared to the extreme debt he had been forgiven. However, he would not forgive the man. He had the debtor thrown into prison until the debt was settled.

> *When the king who had forgiven his debt heard what he done to the man who owed him the one hundred days' wages, he recalled the ten-million-dollar debt. "You wicked servant. I forgave you all that debt, because you begged me. Should you not also have had compassion on your fellow servant just as I had pity on you?"*
> *(Matthew 18:32-33)*

With that, the king commanded the man be put into prison and tortured until he had paid the entire ten million dollars.

Jesus explained the parable to his disciples. "This is how my Heavenly Father will treat each of you unless you forgive your brother from the heart" (Matthew 18:35). Unforgiveness will place a person into a prison of tormentors.

When any individual makes the decision to let the day end with unresolved conflict, unsettled anger or unforgiveness, they give a foothold (area of jurisdiction) to their demonic enemy. The opening for the enemy is present because the grace of God has been rejected. At that point, the individual has committed the same sin as the man in the parable of Jesus.

God extends His grace into a person's life. He willingly forgives all the sin and iniquity that individual has ever committed. However, when the forgiven one is confronted with the sinful act of another, are they willing to extend the same grace? Jesus taught in the Sermon on the Mount, "For if you forgive men their transgressions, your Heavenly Father will also forgive you. But, if you forgive not men, neither will your Heavenly Father forgive your transgressions" (Matthew 6:14-15).

God's grace is not only His benevolent favor toward us when we repent of our sins. It is also the benevolent favor of Almighty God flowing through our life to others. When a person makes the choice not to extend that benevolence, they restrict the working of grace in their own life. That gives fertile ground for bitterness to grow in their heart. The enemy gains a foothold at that point.

A foothold is a place of jurisdiction from which the enemy can send tormentors into a person's life. These tormentors will defile the life of that person with negative emotions, carnal passions of the flesh and self-willed pride. The Apostle Paul wrote to the church at Ephesus as solemn warning about giving the enemy a foothold.

> *"Be angry, and do not sin": do not let the sun go down on your wrath, nor give place to the devil. Let him who stole steal no longer, but rather let him labor, working with his hands what is good, that he may have something to give him who has need. Let no corrupt word proceed out of your mouth, but what is good for necessary edification, that it may impart grace to the hearers. And do not grieve the Holy Spirit of God, by whom you were sealed for the day of redemption. Let all bitterness, wrath, anger, clamor, and evil speaking be put away from you, with all malice. And be kind to*

one another, tenderhearted, forgiving one another, even as God in
Christ forgave you" (Ephesians 4:26-32 NKJV).

Oh, the defilement maybe minor at first. The writer of Hebrews assured us with each passing day the newly planted root of bitterness would grow until "the majority be defiled" (Hebrews 12:15 AMP). Given time, the tormentors will become life controlling agents that determine the personality, character and future of an individual. Dr. Ed Murphy wrote about this spiritual cancer in *The Handbook for Spiritual Warfare.*

> *"Ultimately, as the late Donald Gray Barnhouse writes, Satan is*
> *the primary source of man's terrible sin problem. He writes of*
> *Satan's strategy of seduction with sin. Satan is 'the author of*
> *confusion and lies,' he says. He, 'has done one of his most effective*
> *bits of mystification in creating bewilderment even among many*
> *Christians, concerning his methods of attack.' Barnhouse says,*
> *They are threefold. We do not know what student of the Word of*
> *God first coined the phrase, 'the world, the flesh and the devil,'' he*
> *says. The oldest usage of this tripled division of the field of attack is*
> *to be found in The Book of Common Prayer in prayer for an*
> *infant. 'Grant that he may have power and strength to have victory,*
> *and to triumph, against the devil, the world and flesh'" (p. 103).*

That is the objective of Jesus Christ's completed work of redemption. The Apostle John wrote about our Lord's objective in his first epistle. "He who sins is of the devil, for the devil has sinned from the beginning. For this purpose, the Son of God was manifested that He might destroy the works of the devil" (1John 3:8).

The victory Jesus Christ has won brings joy to the heart and life of everyone who believes. It is that victory that enables an individual to escape the morass of sin and the debilitating power of the tormentors.

Hope for the Human Heart

Jesus was visiting His home town. He had joined the men of Nazareth in the synagogue for prayer and study of the Holy Scriptures. He was asked to read form the scroll. The portion of Scripture appointed to be read for that day was Isaiah 61:1-2. Jesus read, "The Spirit of the Lord is upon Me, because the Lord has anointed Me to preach good tidings to the poor; He has sent me to heal the brokenhearted, to proclaim liberty to the captives, and the opening of prison to those who are bound; to proclaim the acceptable year of the Lord."

After reading the Scripture, Jesus returned the scroll to the attendant and then sat down. Every man looked at him. They were waiting for his comments on the passage. However, they were not expecting the revelation that would be forth coming. "Today," Jesus said, "this Scripture is fulfilled in your hearing (Luke 4:21). The men of Nazareth could not believe what they were hearing. Who was this man to speak such words? What authority did he have to make such a claim? After all, he had grown up among them. He was the Son of Joseph. He could not possibly be the messiah. But, He was! Jesus Christ is the fulfillment of the promised victory Isaiah declared.

Jesus Christ came for the very purposes spoken of by the prophet. He would proclaim good news to the poor. He would heal the brokenhearted. He would declare liberty to the captives. He would proclaim recovery of sight to the blind. He would set at liberty those who were oppressed. He would declare the acceptable year of the Lord.

Each of these declared victories relieves the suffering of mankind and delivers from the dominion of darkness. It breaks the oppression of sin. Jesus Christ declared His mission that day in the synagogue of Nazareth. He had come to "seek and to save that which was lost" (Matthew 18:11). The thief, Satan, had stolen man's dream of purpose and destiny; he killed man's relationship with God; and destroyed his love, joy and peace. Jesus declared, "I have come that you might have life and have it more abundantly" (John 10:10 NKJV). What glorious news for the lost humanity. A Savior has come. A Deliverer has entered the age-long conflict between mankind and the power of evil. A Redeemer has come who can free from the power of sin. A reconciler has intervened who can restore relationship with Almighty God.

The Apostle Paul spoke of this great victory in his letter to the Church of Rome.

> "For if by one man's offense death reigned by one; much more they which receive abundance of grace and of the gift of righteousness shall reign in life by one, Jesus Christ" (Romans 5:17).

Two corresponding truths are presented in this portion of Scripture. Since the transgression of the first man, Adam, death has reigned over all mankind because of the curse of sin. Now, through Jesus Christ, life can reign in the heart of every person who receives Him as Lord and Savior.

Kenneth Wuest says:

> "Sin originated with the angel Lucifer, who in rebelling against God contracted a sinful nature. Adam, in his disobedience was the channel through which sin entered the Human Race" (p. 84).

Lucifer contracted a sinful nature by rebelling against God. When Adam yielded to deception of the serpent, he followed in Lucifer's footsteps, rebelled against God and contracted a sinful nature. Adam's sinful nature has been passed down from generation to generation throughout the human race. Adam also enslaved mankind to Satan, the prince of darkness.

> *"Do you not know that to whom you present yourselves slaves to obey, you are that one's slaves whom you obey whether of sin leading to death, or of obedience leading to righteousness" (Romans 6:16 NKJV).*

When Adam disobeyed God, he unwittingly subjected himself and his descendants to the slavery of sin and Satan. The entire human race carries the curse of sin. "God looks down from heaven upon the children of men to see if there are any who understand, who seek God. Every one of them has turned aside; they have together become corrupt; there is none who does good, no not one" (Psalm 53:2-3 NKJV).

The Greek word for "slave" in Romans 6:16, ("servants to obey") is *doulos*. It comes from the Greek word, *deyo* that means, to tie or to bind. *Doulos* means someone who is bound to another person or a slave. The word was used in Greek literature referring to someone in a servile condition totally given up to the will of another.

A *doulos* was born into slavery with no will of their own. They lived totally under the will of another person. They served their master with total disregard to their own interests and desire. The only means for a *doulos* to be free from slavery was death.

This, says the Apostle Paul, is the condition of the natural born human being. Mankind is hopelessly, helplessly and habitually a sinner. We are so bound to this slavery we can do nothing to free ourselves, except death. "The wages of sin is death" (Romans 6:23 KJV). All sinners will find themselves eternally bound to the master of darkness in hell's flaming torment.

While the "wages of sin is death" the "gift of God is eternal life through Jesus Christ our Lord" (Romans 6:23). Jesus Christ has provided a way of escape from the unbreakable bondage of slavery. Jesus Christ died in our place. He paid the price of death, so we could receive the gift of grace and freedom from slavery to sin. "It was for freedom that Christ has made us free" (Galatians 5:1 NAS).

The Apostle Paul describes this wonderful freedom to the believers living in Colossae.

> *"He [Jesus Christ] has delivered us from the power of darkness and conveyed us into the kingdom of the Son of His love, in whom we have redemption through His blood, the forgiveness of sins" (Colossians 1:13-14 KJV).*

The amazing and wonderful truth is every human being can be free from the power of sin. They can enjoy true liberty. Dr. Bill Gothard has said, "True freedom is the freedom to live right." Each person can now be at peace with God, with his own conscience, and with men and women living around them. All of this made possible through Jesus Christ's betrayal, arrest, false trials, torture, and crucifixion.

"Know ye not that so many of us as we baptized into Jesus Christ
were baptized into His death. Therefore, being buried with Him by
baptism into death, that like as Christ was raised up from the dead
by the glory of the Father, even so we also should walk in newness of
life. For, if we have been planted together in the likeness of His
death, we shall be also in the likeness of His resurrection. Knowing
this, that our old man is crucified with Him that the body of sin
might be destroyed that henceforth we should not serve sin. For he
that is dead is freed from sin" (Romans 6:3-7 KJV).

The death, burial and resurrection of Jesus Christ have broken the power of sin and have made new life possible for every person. The Apostle Peter explained in his second epistle. "Whereby are given unto us exceeding great and precious promises, that by these, we might be partakers of the divine nature having escaped the corruption that is the world through lust" (2 Peter 1:4 KJV).

Jesus referred to this same life changing miracle in His conversation with a Jewish religious leader, Nicodemus, "Most assuredly I say to you, unless one is born of water and the spirit, he cannot enter the kingdom of God. That which is born of the flesh is flesh and that which is born of the Spirit is spirit" (John 3:5-6 NKJV).

Spiritual birth makes it possible for a whole new life to arise with a person. It gives them a new heart with a new motivation for living. "Therefore, if any man [person] be in Christ, he is a new creature, old things are passed away and behold, all things are become new; and all things are of God" (2 Corinthians 5:17 KJV).

When a person recognizes their life of sin and asks God to forgiven them and invites Jesus Christ to come live in their heart, they will experience a new birth. Jesus will give them a whole new life. Living in the power and freedom of that new life will come through identification with the full work Jesus Christ accomplished through His death burial and resurrection.

It is a miracle that happens through the power of the Holy Spirit and the Word of God in a person's life. No amount of self-help training will accomplish this life change. Psychology and psychiatry are beneficial but fall dreadfully short of giving a new heart and a new life. Twelve-step accountability groups are encouraging and beneficial, as far as they can go; but can do nothing more that leave the individual living the remainder of their life confessing they are in slavery to an addictive nature.

The victory Jesus Christ won proclaims the individual a "new creation." The power of the Gospel of Jesus Christ is in its ability to give a new heart and a new source of living. The same Holy Spirit that raised Jesus Christ from the dead fills their heart and empowers them to live free from the slavery of the addictive nature; free from the debilitating memories of past abuses, wounds and hurts; free from the condemnation, shame and humiliation of former behaviors.

"But if the Spirit of Him who raised Jesus from the dead dwells in you, He who raised Christ Jesus from the dead will also give life to your mortal bodies through His Spirit who dwells in you. So then, brethren, we are under obligation, not to the flesh, to live according to the flesh — for if you are living according to the flesh, you must die; but if by the Spirit you are putting to death the deeds of the

body, you will live. For all who are being led by the Spirit of God, these are sons of God. For you have not received a spirit of slavery leading to fear again, but you have received a spirit of adoption as sons by which we cry out, " Abba! Father!" (Romans 8:11-15 NAS).

Out of this new heart will flow abundant living and freedom. They will receive a renewed mind, refocused emotions, and a redirected will, enabling them to live the new life where their past and present circumstances do not have to determine their future or their identity. Their identity now comes from their life in Jesus Christ. Their past is dead and buried and no longer lives. Their current circumstances do not mean that is the way they have to live. They are a new person living an abundant, victorious life.

When I first met the man he has just moved to the city where I was living and serving as pastor. He wore a beard to his waist and his hair hung to his waist. He lived in an apartment with another young man and that man's girlfriend.

He had grown up in a Christian home but had rejected Christianity and began using drugs while in high school. He was a very gifted musician and had played in some of the leading rock bands in the United States. He was a functioning alcoholic and drug addict. He rarely missed a day of work. He also rarely worked a day sober. His addictions cost him dearly. He used $1500.00 a week in drugs and another $500.00 a week in alcohol.
The man's spiritual journey had taken him through eastern mysticism and a variety of new age genres. His journey through this maze of darkness left him empty and still searching. His godly mother and sister prayed earnestly for him. They prayed God would bring him back to the truth and freedom of Jesus Christ. That day came in 1981.

An outreach team from our local congregation called on their home one day. I was asked to make a return visit with them the following week. During that second visit the man and his two roommates received Jesus Christ as Lord and Savior.

The power of the Jesus Christ and the Holy Spirit broke his addiction to narcotics immediately. A week late the power of alcohol was broken. He began to read the entire New Testament through every week. His mind was fully stored in six months.

I had the joy of officiating as his wedding one year later. He entered full time Christian ministry in 1983. The power of amazing Freedom!

The Power of Identification

The Apostle Paul asked an insightful question in Romans 6:1. It is a question each believer needs to ask themselves. "Shall we [shall I] continue in sin?" Should I continue living controlled by fear? Should I continue living depressed? Should I continue abusing my family with my temper? Should I continue secretly viewing pornography? Should I continue controlling my mate with jealousy? The Apostle's question is vital to every believer's life.

The Apostle answers his own question with an astounding and adamant statement. "God forbid!" May it never be!", one translation says.

Another question is begging to be asked. Does God only forgive sin? Does He give the believer power to live in victory over the sin that once imprisoned and dominated their life?

God does not save someone and then leave them as a POW or an MIA. God causes His children to triumph always in Jesus Christ (2 Corinthians 2:14). The child of God is never at the mercy of the enemy or the circumstances of life. They are never left to deal with temptation, habits or emotions with powerless inability. God has given a promise. There is "no temptation overtaken you except such as is common to man; but God is faithful, who will not allow you to be tempted beyond what you are able, but with the temptation will also make a way of escape, that you may be able to bear it" (1 Corinthians 10:13 KJV).

The source of victorious Christian living is found in identification, "That I might know Him and the power of His resurrection and the fellowship of His sufferings, being made comfortable unto His death" (Philippians 3:10). It is identification with the suffering of Jesus Christ and the empowerment of the same Holy Spirit that raised Jesus from the dead.

"Likewise, you also, reckon yourselves to be dead indeed to sin, but alive unto God through Jesus Christ our Lord" (Romans 6:11). The word "reckon" in Greek is *logizomai*. It is an accountant's term meaning to take account or to compute. The believer is to debit his life's account as being dead to sin and alive to God. The Apostle Paul also used this bookkeeping term in 2 Corinthians 5:19. "That is, God was in Christ reconciling the world to Himself, not imputing their trespasses to them, and has committed to us the word of reconciliation." The word "imputing" is *logizomai*. When a person has been born again in Jesus Christ his old life has passed away. Everything has become new. God removed all accounts of past sins declaring the person *justified*.

God held court in heaven with Jesus Christ as the defense attorney. On the basis of the all sufficient sacrifice of Jesus Christ, God declares the sinner not guilty and their former life to be dead and buried to live no more. Heavenly Father orders all records of the former life to be destroyed and proclaims the individual to be righteous and holy in Jesus Christ" (2 Corinthians 5:17-21; Hebrews 10:15-17).

There is some accounting work the believer must also do if there is to be a successful carrying out of the transaction. The believer must choose to identify with all God has declared them to be in Christ Jesus. They must "reckon" in their own heart they are indeed dead to sin and alive to God. It is an act of the will based upon absolute trust and confidence in the completed work of Jesus Christ.

Identification is choosing to accept a new image of personal identity. It is an image based upon our identity in Christ Jesus. The individual no longer sees themselves based upon their life before receiving Jesus Christ as Savior and Lord or their natural birth heritage. They identify with the new creature in Jesus Christ. Through new birth, they have been given a new heart and a new identity. This must become the image by which they choose to see themselves and live their life. It is based upon the three-fold work of Jesus Christ.

The Apostle Paul wrote to the Church in Rome, "Knowing this, that our old man is crucified with Him, that the body of sin might be done away with..." (Romans 6:6 NKJV). The Apostle was referring to the crucifixion of Jesus Christ. The Roman soldier laid Jesus across the beam of wood and drove nails into each wrist. Then placing one foot upon the other, he drove a single nail into the feet. At that moment the sin of all humanity came upon Jesus. The soldier was not only nailing Jesus Christ to the cross. Unknown to him, he was nailing the records of every sin committed by each person onto that cross. He was nailing the judgment written against every human being onto that cross. As Jesus Christ hung on that cross suffering its pain and humiliation, He was paying the penalty of every sin every recorded by human history (Colossians 2:13-14). It is impossible for the natural mind to comprehend the weight and the horror of such suffering. The physical pain of crucifixion is not imaginable. The combination of crucifixion and carrying the penalty of mankind's sin is unfathomable. "And the Lord has laid on Him the iniquity of us all (Isaiah 53:6 NKJV). Jesus Christ became sin for you and me so we could become the righteousness of God (2 Corinthians 5:21). Thus, our

39

former life of sin, pain and suffering is dead and the strength and power of it to control our life and establish our identity is removed.

The Apostle continued his exhortation to the Church in Rome, "Or do you not know that as many of us as were baptized into Christ Jesus, were baptized into His death" (Romans 6:3 NKJV)? After his death, Jesus body was removed from the cross and buried in a borrowed tomb. Joseph of Arimathea owned a vineyard near to the place of crucifixion. In the vineyard was a burial tomb he had prepared for his family. He requested permission from the Roman authorities to bury the body of Jesus in his family tomb. Permission was granted. The burial was hastily carried out because it was Sabbath eve. The company of family and friends did not understand the spiritual significance of their hasty work. Sadly, many believers do not understand the significance either.

When the women hastily perfumed and wrapped Jesus body in the grave cloths they were wrapping the sins of all humanity in those cloths as well. When the men carried the body into the tomb and laid it on the burial shelf, the sins of all mankind were laid in the tomb with Jesus. Colossians 2:11-13 proclaims when a believer identifies with Jesus Christ's burial they experience spiritual circumcision that removes all identity and influence of the old sinful life. That is only possible because the sin of each person was crucified with Jesus Christ and then buried with Him to live no longer.

Sunday morning, following the hasty burial of Jesus, a group of women returned to the garden tomb to complete the entombment. When they arrived at the burial site they found the body was gone. Jesus Christ had risen from the dead. They quickly ran back to the other disciples to tell them the news. Peter and John in wonder and great concern immediately ran to the tomb.

John, being younger, ran faster than Peter and arrived at the tomb first. He stopped and was looking into the tomb when Peter arrived. Peter did not stop outside but went in to inspect the burial shelf. What did these disciples find?

The body of Jesus was gone, but the burial cloths were remained in the tomb lying on the burial shelf. Why is it significant that Jesus did not wear the burial cloths out of the tomb? Because wrapped in those burial cloths were the sins of mankind and the judgments written against each person.

Jesus Christ has risen, indeed, but the sins of mankind remain buried in the tomb to live no more. Every person can live a new life free from sin, condemnation and the guilt and pain of the past. Their former life is dead and buried with Jesus Christ and no longer lives. When Jesus Christ rose from the dead they rose to new life with Him. Now, "If the Spirit of Him who raised Jesus from the dead is living in you, He who raised Christ from the dead will also give life to your mortal bodies through His Spirit who lives in you" (Romans 8:11 NIV).

This wonderful promise was given by God to Jeremiah the prophet (Jeremiah 31:33-34) and was repeated by the writer of Hebrews (Hebrews 10:15-17). "And the Holy Spirit also bears witness to us; for after saying, 'This is the covenant that I will make with them after those days, says the Lord: I will put My laws upon their heart, and upon their mind I will write them,' [He then says] 'and their sins and their lawless deeds I will remember no more'" (NAS).

When an individual accepts Jesus Christ as Lord and Savior, the sins of their life are forgiven and the accounts are dismissed. All records are wiped clean. All guilt is dismissed. All spiritual responsibility and accountability for those actions have been taken away forever. All shame and humiliation have been removed. The sins of that individual were buried with Jesus Christ never to live again. "therefore, we were buried with Him through baptism into death, that just as Christ was raised up from the dead by the glory of the Father, even so, we should walk in newness of life" (Romans 6:4 NKJV), resurrection power and life lives within the believer.

The same Holy Spirit that raised Jesus Christ from the dead comes and lives in the heart of every person who receives Jesus Christ into their heart. "Therefore," the Apostle Paul urges every believer, "Brothers, we have an obligation-but it is not to the sinful nature, to live according to it. For if you live according to the sinful nature, you will die; but if by the Spirit you put to death the misdeeds of the body, you will live, because those who are led by the Spirit of God are sons of God. For you did not receive a spirit that makes you a slave again to fear, but you received the Spirit of sonship. And by him we cry, "Abba, Father." The Spirit himself testifies with our spirit that we are God's children" (Romans 8:12-16 NIV).

That is why the Apostle wrote, "Therefore do not let sin reign in your mortal body so that you obey its evil desires. Do not offer the parts of your body to sin, as instruments of wickedness, but rather offer yourselves to God, as those who have been brought from death to life; and offer the parts of your body to him as instruments of righteousness. For sin shall not be your master, because you are not under law, but under grace" (Romans 6:12-14 NIV).

The controlling power of former habits can be broken. A person no longer need be subject to their old behavior. Painful memories and past hurts do not have to be disabling. A person's future and their destiny do not have to be determined by their past experiences or their former lifestyle. The power of God's grace has delivered mankind from the rule and the dominion of sin.

The individual must choose to access the miraculous power of grace into his or her life.

The Dynamic of a Renewed Mind

The ability to live each day with purpose and destiny comes from the dynamic of new thinking and positive emotions. The Apostle Paul dealt with this in his writings to the church in Ephesus.

> "This I say, therefore, and testify in the Lord, that you should no longer walk as the rest of the Gentiles walk, in the futility of their mind, having their understanding darkened, being alienated from the life of God, because of the ignorance that is in them, because of the blindness of their heart; who, being past feeling, have given themselves over to lewdness, to work all uncleanness with greediness. But you have not so learned Christ, if indeed you have heard Him and have been taught by Him, as the truth is in Jesus: that you put off, concerning your former conduct, the old man which grows corrupt according to the deceitful lusts, and be renewed in the spirit of your mind, and that you put on the new man which was created according to God, in true righteousness and holiness" (Ephesians 4:17-24 NKJV).

Abundant life begins with new birth by the power of the Holy Spirit. The daily experience of enjoying abundant living requires the transforming work of the Holy Spirit within the mind of the believer. This work of the Holy

Spirit allows the expression of the fruit of the Spirit; love, joy, peace, longsuffering, gentleness, goodness, faith, meekness, and temperance to be manifest in the believer's life (Galatians 5:22-23). It releases the power to live in victory over the hold habits and behavior patterns.

The Apostle Paul addressed this very important aspect of the believer's life in Romans 12:2. "And be not conformed to this world, but be transformed by the renewing of the mind, that you may prove what is that good and accept and perfect will of God."

The Apostle was urging the believer to not be shaped or controlled by the philosophies, culture, ideologies of the world around them. Their life must reflect the clear will of God. This happens when the transforming power of the Holy Spirit renews the mind. The Greek word for "transformed" is *metamorphoooomai*. The English word metamorphosis is derived from this Greek word. Metamorphosis means "a change of form, structure, substance or function," according to Webster's New World Dictionary (Neufeldt, 1990). Metamorphosis is that life transformation that changes a wooly worm into a butterfly or a tadpole into a bullfrog. "Bull frogs and butterflies have both been born again," sang Barry McGuire.

There is a spiritual metamorphosis that must take place in the life of a person. A wooly worm changes its "form, structure, substance and function" from that of a wiggly and fuzzy worm, that frightens little girls, into a beautiful and graceful Monarch. Once controlled by ungodly thinking, negative emotions and carnal appetites, a person can be transformed into a saint of God; filled with righteous thinking and the fruit of the Holy Spirit.

The miraculous transformation is made possible by the "renewing of the mind." The Greek word for "renewing" is *anakainosis*. Kenneth Wuest describes the work of renewing as "the gradual conforming of the man more and more to that new spiritual world into which he has been introduced, and in which he now lives and moves; the restoration of the divine image; and in all this so far from being passive, he must be a fellow-worker with God" (Wuest, 208).

Living the abundant life requires a person's mind be made like the mind of Christ (Philippians 2:5). The conscious and the subconscious mind of a believer must be transformed if they are to live in the dynamic of new life. The old thought patterns must be changed into the way God thinks. The value systems, philosophies, ideologies, and reasoning of a person must be adjusted so they match the ways of God. The memory patterns and dream life of the old man must be renovated to conform to the truth of God.

If the mind of a person is transformed to think and reason by the mind of Christ, that individual will view life and daily circumstances from God's perspective. They will refocus their emotions to agree with the truth of God's Word. Instead of living as a victim, they live in victory. Instead of being held in fear, worry, and insecurity, they will have a positive outlook. Rather than responding to people with rejection, jealousy and low self-worth, they accept themselves in the image of Jesus Christ. Instead of being captive to their old habits and behavior patterns, they "stand fast in the liberty by which Christ has made [them] free" (Galatians 5:1 NKJV).

The daily application of such freedom is made possible by the sufferings of Jesus Christ. Each point of His suffering has purchased for us a place of victory. Jesus wrestled alone in the Garden of Gethsemane sweating great drops of blood. He won the victory by yielding to the will of God. Now mankind can surrender his will to the will of God in the most difficult of moments (Matthew 26:36-46).

Jesus was betrayed by the kiss of a close friend, one of his disciples. He won the victory over bitterness through mercy and grace. Now every person who experiences betrayal can be victorious over bitterness in their moment of broken trust (Matthew 26:47-50).

Jesus was taken captive by the religious authorities. He was unjustly placed on trial, abused and imprisoned in the house of the High Priest. Christ won the victory over religious bigotry and false accusations through speaking truth. Now all who have been held captive by the traditions of men and religious rituals can be released from the bondage of legalism and condemnation (Matthew 26:57-68).

Jesus was found innocent by the Roman governor, Pontius Pilate. The governor yielded to political pressure and Pilate ordered Jesus beaten and crucified. Our Lord won the victory by silently suffering through the accusations and torture. Now all who suffer unjust accusations and false reports can live free from resentment and continually having to defend themselves (Luke 23:13-15).

Jesus was rejected by the crowds. They chose a murderer named Barabbas instead of the innocent Son of God. Jesus won this victory by showing love and mercy. He chose to go to the cross in our place. Now all who suffer rejection, abuse and low self-worth can receive a new identity as a new creation in Jesus Christ (Matthew 27:15-26; 2 Corinthians 5:17).

Jesus Christ was unjustly flogged at the whipping post. He won the victory by carrying in His own body the "griefs" (sickness) and "sorrows" (pain) of all people (Isaiah 53:3-4). Jesus was literally suffering all the sickness and pain mankind would ever suffer. Now all who live in pain, suffer disease, experience hurt, or are emotionally wounded can be healed.

The Roman soldiers placed a crown of thorns on Jesus and pulled out His beard. They placed robe on Him and knelt at His feet mocking Him as royalty. Christ won the victory by submitting Himself to the righteous judgment of Almighty God. Now every person who suffers the torment of negative thinking, fear, worry, or anxiety can live in the victory of a renewed mind and refocused emotions (Matthew 27:27-31; 1 Peter 2:23).

While handing on the cross of Calvary, Jesus was continually accused and mocked. Christ won the victory by forgiving those who accused and mocked. He also forgave one of the thieves hanging on a cross beside Him and promised the man eternal life. Now all mankind can live victorious over the continual accusations of the "accuser of the brethren" (Matthew 27:33-38; Luke 23:39-43).

Nails were driven through the hands and feet of the Son of God. Jesus Christ forgave those who unjustly crucified Him. Now every person can be free from the judgment of violating the Commandments of God and sinful behavior (Matthew 27:32-37).

Jesus died on the cross and won the victory of sin, "for the wages of sin is death." When Jesus died the veil in the temple, separating the Holy Sanctuary from the Holiest of All (the very presence of God) was torn. Now every person can be forgiven of their sins and enjoy free access to the Living presence of God (Matthew 27:45-55; Hebrews 10:15-19).

Jesus was buried in a borrowed tomb. He won the victory over death by raising from the dead on the third day. Now all of mankind can experience eternal life through in Jesus Christ and His death, burial and resurrection (John 3:16).

Jesus Christ has won a great and momentous victory for the human race. Each person must access that victory for themselves. It does not just happen automatically. It is not experienced because a person is born in America or grows up in a Christian home. It does not happen in a person's life because they attend church regularly or read their Bible and pray every day. The power of Christ's victory is experienced through personal repentance and identification with His resurrection life. Every person who experience new birth can live a victorious Christ life through identifying, by faith, they were in Christ when He experienced all of the suffering.

The Glory of Living Free

Fear gripped the young lady's heart as she began to share the pain and trauma of her life. She was a stunningly beautiful woman in her twenties who lived daily with horror of her childhood. When she was but a small child an uncle began making uninvited and unwanted visits to her bedroom. These nightly experiences of sexual abuse continued until she was out of high school.

She was traumatized and filled with hate. The gentlest of touches from a man's hand to her hand sent her body into convulsions. She could never feel clean, no matter how many showers she took. The memory of each visit filled her with torment day and night. Tormenting questions flooded her mind: "Why would God do this to me?" "Why is God punishing me?" "What evil did I do as a child?" and the question that drove her to attend the seminar, "Why can't I be normal?"

I led her through an explanation of Christ's completed work through His suffering. Holy Spirit revealed to her God's all sufficient grace. Slowly a spiritual awakening began in her heart. The defilement of her spirit was cleansed. Worth and value began to spring up within her. The prison door of hate and bitterness was thrown open, and she walked out into a whole new world. The chains of rejection and low self-worth were broken off, allowing her to accept a new identity. The torments of guilt, fear, worry and insecurity were banished, and she experienced the new emotions of love, joy, peace and hope.

A person's past or present circumstances do not have to determine their future or their identity. Their birth circumstances or the home life in which they were raised does not have to determine their behavior or their identity. A person does not have to be the product of their environment or a victim of their parent's addictions. A child growing up in an abusive home is not predestined to be abusive.

Jesus Christ makes it possible to live free from these life-determining conditions.

> *"Therefore, if any man is in Christ, he is a new creature; the old things passed away; behold, new things have come. Now all these things are from God, who reconciled us to Himself through Christ, and gave us the ministry of reconciliation" (2 Corinthians 5:17 NAS).*

Mankind is no longer trapped by circumstances of life. Family heritage, nationality, socio-economic conditions, or a life of sin do not have to determine a person's life style or behavior patterns. God has made it possible for each person to be released from the sin nature by being born again through in Jesus Christ. The re-creative power of new birth gives each individual the potential of living a life with a renewed mind, refocused emotions and a reshaped will. Indeed, the life change can be so complete the character and personality of the person is transformed. As the Scripture says, "He is a new creature." The power of the Holy Spirit makes that person a new creation. The Apostle Peter declares the have become "partakers of the divine nature, having escaped the corruption that is in the world through lust" (2 Peter 1:4).

New birth through Jesus Christ is the only hope mankind has for overcoming the morass into which he is sinking. Psychology or psychiatry have failed in their attempt to heal the troubled mind and broken emotions of man. Educational and social reform have miserably failed to lift American, European, or any other society out of the depravity into which it is plummeting. The question must be asked, "Why?"

It certainly is not because education or psychology is not needed. It is not for lack of sincerity. It is not because everything they do is wrong. In most cases, the failure can be traced to the insufficiency of education, socio-economic reform and the science of psychology.

The important element left out in each case is the redemptive work of Jesus Christ. True life change does not come through education, social reform, economic reform, counseling, or psycho-therapy alone. If true life change is to take place, there must be the element of heart change. Education without heart change will only enable the sinner to be more intelligent and creative in their pursuit of evil. Social reform without heart change dresses the community in new paint, better housing, higher income, but leaves the root of the social evil in place.

The basic nature of the people living in the community is unchanged. Counseling, without heart change, surfaces the memory of experienced pain, past wounds and behavioral disorders. It may even identify the causes for addictive or abnormal behavior. It is endeavoring to heal damaged emotions without the one who was "wounded for our transgressions and bruised for our iniquities." They are seeking to bring inner tranquility and serenity without the one who carried the "chastisement of our peace." They offer healing without the one of whom it is said, "By His stripes we are healed."

The believers must give to the community more than religious education. They must do more than offer social reform to the city. The pastors must offer more than psychology in the counseling appointment. God has given to the church the most life changing power known to mankind. The believer must learn to minister the power God has given with skill and effectiveness. The education and teaching of the Church must make true disciples of Jesus Christ. Opportunity should be given for them to personally experience the life changing power of new birth and the renewing of the mind. Then teach and train the follower of Jesus how to minister the same to others.

The social ministry of the Church should also give each recipient of the social service the life changing ministry of Jesus' death, burial and resurrection. Food, clothing and shelter should be offered with no strings attached. These ministries must be done on the merit of their value in obedience to Jesus' command. These ministries must also be done in the redemptive spirit, not just providing for the physical need. This generation needs mentoring programs, homes for unwed mothers and addiction recovery centers. However, with each of these ministries opportunity must also be provided for each person to experience the heart changing power of the Gospel of Jesus Christ. It alone gives true hope and life purpose.

The counseling arm of ministry has suffered the most in recent decades. The majority of Christian counseling is now based upon the presuppositions of psychology. These presuppositions have their roots in the work of Freud, Rogers, Skinner, Mower, Glasser and other researchers. Some measure of truth may be found in each. However, they approach the problems of man from the humanistic world view that man is basically good. They predominately use a medical model for resolving the problems of man. They seek to help a person discover the solution to life's problems from within themselves. These are exactly the opposite from the Gospel of Jesus Christ and some even oppose the truth of God's Word.

This leaves the believer giving the same answers the world offers to people in need. This must not be! We have the answers no one else can give. Jesus Christ won the victory! Every person can now live life free from the bondages and slavery that plagues the human race. They can live with healthy minds, whole emotions, good relationships, and with purpose and destiny. This is the message of the Holy Scriptures.

It is vital that every believer understands clearly the work Jesus has completed for this victory and the healing it brings. It is a finished work! "Therefore, He is able to save to the uttermost-completely, perfectly, finally and for all time and eternity-those who come to God through Him since He is always living to make petition to God and intercede with Him and intervene for them" (Hebrews 7:25 AMP).

The believer must know how to access and to apply the life-changing power and victories Jesus Christ has won. The making of a disciple happens in this process. The believer should not only learn how to apply the victory to their own life but help another person learn to renew their mind so they can think as Jesus thinks; so they can refocus their emotions; so they are filled with the fruit of the Holy Spirit; and so they can see themselves as a new creation in Jesus Christ with a new life and a new identity. The true disciple of Jesus Christ learns to live each day facing the circumstances of life from these perspectives. That is abundant living and that is *Discovering True Identity!*

More Books from Dr. Hackett

The Freedom Series:

Agape

Charis

The Disciples Series:

Discovering Jesus

The Joy of Becoming Like Jesus

Becoming Ambassadors for Christ

A Gift for You

Receive a free Bible reading plan and journal each month when you visit Foundational at fdeanhackett.com. At Foundational, we are passionate about getting families in Word of God and want to partner with you in building a strong foundation for future generations!

About Foundational

If you were inspired by Discovering True Identity and would like more information about how you can establish your identity in Jesus Christ, I encourage you to connect with Foundational. Foundational exists to help you build a strong foundation in your life and in the lives of your children so that we can raise up future generations that live passionately for Jesus Chirst.

To learn more about Foundational, you can contact us at dean@fdeanhackett.com, or visit fdeanhackett.com